Successful
E-Commerce

in a week

DAVE HOWELL

GW00692144

Hodder & Stoughton

A MEMBER OF THE HODDER HEADLINE GROUP

in the Institute of Management

The Institute of Management (IM) is the leading
organisation for professional management.
Its purpose is to promote the art and science of
management in every sector and at every level,
through research, education, training and
development, and representation of members'
views on management issues.

This series is commissioned by IM Enterprises
Limited, a subsidiary of the Institute of Management,
providing commercial services.

Management House,
Cottingham Road,
Corby,
Northants NN17 1TT
Tel: 01536 204222;
Fax: 01536 201651
Website: http://www.inst-mgt.org.uk

Registered in England no 3834492
Registered office: 2 Savoy Court, Strand,
London WC2R 0EZ

Orders: please contact Bookpoint Ltd, 39 Milton Park, Abingdon, Oxon OX14 4TD. Telephone:
(44) 01235 400414, Fax: (44) 01235 400454. Lines are open from 9.00 - 6.00, Monday to Saturday,
with a 24 hour message answering service.
Email address: orders@bookpoint.co.uk

British Library Cataloguing in Publication Data
A catalogue record for this title is available from The British Library

ISBN 0 340 753366

First published 1999
Impression number   10 9 8 7 6 5 4 3 2
Year   2005 2004 2003 2002 2001 2000 1999

Cover photo from TCL Stock Directory.
Typeset by Multiplex Techniques Ltd, St Mary Cray, Kent.
Printed in Great Britain for Hodder & Stoughton Educational, a division of
Hodder Headline Plc, 338 Euston Road, London NW1 3BH by Cox & Wyman Ltd, Reading,
Berkshire.

■ I N T R O D U C T I O N ■

Business today faces a challenge. Digital TV is now a reality, and with it the last barrier to easy and affordable access to online content has been swept away. Now, anyone with a TV will shortly be able to access the Internet for information, entertainment, but more importantly as a means of making purchases. By the turn of the century the technology will be in place to bring customers to the website of any business, where they can freely make purchases as they now do in the high street.

The new online marketplace is one that is about to explode. Any business that doesn't sit up and take notice of this new economic landscape will be left behind by their competitors. The consumer will embrace this new buying experience as they did with mail order purchases, but online shopping offers a new level of customer empowerment that all merchants, large and small, must take note of.

As the millennium comes to a close, the elements of a global marketplace are falling into place. In *Successful E-commerce in a Week* you will see how you can move your business onto the Internet and develop a strategy for online trading that will be in place once this new market becomes fully active and established. Over the next seven days you will see how you can:

- Embrace this new economic landscape
- Implement an E-commerce strategy
- Choose an electronic shop front
- Consider your legal position
- Understand your business' place in this global market

Now is the time to act.

What is E-commerce?

The new buzz word at the end of the 90s is E-commerce. To some degree every business does some kind of electronic business. Orders taken via phone or fax are primitive forms of E-commerce. The definition here, however, refers to the use of electronic networks as a means of making transactions, either between businesses or direct to customers. Electronic transactions have been made for some years.

- Large retailers use a system called EDI (Electronic Data Interchange)
- Large financial institutions move assets electronically
- Billions of pounds move electronically between the UK's banks each day.

The use of these electronic systems has one major drawback: they are very expensive to implement. E-commerce as we know it today relies on another major development: the Internet. Beginning life in the academic world, it was little known until the World Wide Web came

into existence along with the first Internet browser, Netscape's Navigator. This put a user-friendly face on what was an archaic communications system, and opened this up for use by anyone that had access to a computer.

Here was a cheap means of connecting computers and, therefore, people together. The networks were primarily used to move text messages from machine to machine. These networks have grown exponentially over the last few years; as a result the potential customer base has mushroomed. The turn of the century will see this market come into its own, and will eventually eclipse the merchant/customer relationship that now exists via retail outlets in the physical world.

At the moment the established markets have staggering statistics attached to them. The US market is the benchmark. It is expected that these kinds of statistics will soon apply to the online marketplace.

- 82 billion transactions a year are completed in the USA. Of these:
  - 35 billion are cash sales
  - 33 billion are cheque sales
  - 12 billion are credit card sales
- business writes about 30 billion cheques a year.

(Source: *The Future of the Electronic Marketplace.* MIT Press.)

Why move your business to the Internet?

A revolution is taking place. Business is about to be transformed on many levels, but the most fundamental aspect will be the way in which it sells to its customers. E-commerce offers an opportunity that cannot be missed.

A clear misconception has, however, developed that E-commerce is a large and expensive undertaking that is only suitable for large corporations. Nothing could be further from the truth. The Internet, and doing business online, can be as inexpensive as you would like to make it. On Wednesday you will see that there are electronic shop fronts to suit all needs and budgets.

The move to the Internet and an E-commerce solution offer a number of clear advantages to any business.

- *The chance to compete with all your competitors.* Previously, business existed in a niche. Each business competed with companies of similar size. The Internet is a level playing field.
- *The possibility to cut costs, in some cases to negligible amounts.* British Airways, for instance, saves on average £7 on overhead costs each time a ticket is booked online.
- Administration becomes more streamlined as order processing and billing are all done electronically and simultaneously.
- An existing business model like a mail order catalogue can easily be adapted to online commerce.
- Via the Internet any business can reach new customers that it had not previously been able to sell to.

What are the strengths and weaknesses of this move?

Businesses must not make the mistake that moving even a small part of their operation to the Internet will bring instant wealth. As with any move into a new market, the pros and cons of that move must be evaluated carefully if costly mistakes are to be avoided. On Saturday you will see that you must build into your Action Plan proper costings for the setting up and maintenance of your website; only then can you begin to contemplate an economic success which provides your business with another permanent income.

Strengths
- A business that only trades in their own country now has the opportunity to trade globally
- An existing customer base can be enhanced with additional services provided via the Internet
- Brand presence can be developed
- Direct communication with customers is facilitated
- Fulfilment processes are streamlined

- Marketing can be more focused when an online business uses its sales demographics and customer profiles, all of which can be generated online.

Weaknesses

- The size of the Internet can make it difficult for a store to stand out without expensive media campaigns
- Trading globally with multiple currencies can be difficult
- Cultural differences are often overlooked on the Net i.e., a business must ensure it is trading legally in those markets which it is likely to reach
- Multiple language support: the Internet is global and English may be the universal language, but businesses must take into account that a large proportion of their potential business may not speak English
- Delivery of tangible goods must be as efficient in the global market place as it is in the business' home country – smaller businesses may find this particularly difficult (we will look at this point in detail on Friday)
- Many existing customers may not yet have easy access to the Internet and, therefore, a business' website.

How can E-commerce benefit your business?

Failure to appreciate how the Internet and E-commerce can enhance a business' profitability is the fundamental reason why many businesses are failing to take advantage of this new marketplace. The Internet and E-commerce is not just for technology based companies. Any business can benefit. Yet some business leaders cannot see how their business models fit into this new economic landscape. This is, however, the very heart of the problem. Existing business models do not apply. A business must transform not only the way it does business with its clients, but also the way that it is organised to take the maximum advantage of E-commerce.

If you can answer yes to any of the questions below, your business can benefit from E-commerce.

- Do you sell a product(s) that can be easily shipped to customers?
- Does your business primarily sell information?
- Do you offer customer support via telephone at the moment?
- Are you constrained by limited advertising budgets?
- Do you publish a printed catalogue?
- Are your goods or services specialised?

Integrating E-commerce into an existing website

Many businesses may have already taken the plunge and set up a website. In most cases this has been somewhat of a knee jerk reaction to the media coverage of the Internet, and partly as a reaction to business competitors appearing online. No one wants to be left behind when staking a claim in this new marketplace.

An existing website can easily be adapted to offer E-commerce services to its customers. The route that is taken will largely depend on how a business has organised its website, what kind of goods or services it sells, and how comprehensive it wants its order fulfilment to be. Simply taking orders via e-mail is the simplest method, but your customers will quickly tire of sending repetitive messages each time they wish to order an item. E-commerce should be transparent, trouble free, and as easy (if not easier) than buying the goods in the high street.

Businesses have a number of options when adding an E-commerce solution to an existing website:

- a new shop front
- adding a payment option

A new shop front
In many cases the website of a business will contain a database of the goods for sale. Software such as *Shop@ssistant* offers a simple means of moving your existing database of goods onto an E-commerce ready website.

Shop@ssistant (covered in greater detail on Wednesday) offers a means of taking your existing database and creating your shop front from this information. *NetStart* is the shop front software from the leading payment company NetBanx which we will look at on Tuesday when we look at online payment systems. Here a series of simple forms allows a company to build its E-commerce compatible website quickly. *NetStart's* key features are:

- multiple catalogue pages
- multiple item selection
- individual item prices (including shipping and VAT)
- area banded shipping costs by weight or unit
- order or item discounting
- stock maintenance.

Adding a payment option
On Tuesday you will see how the major players in the online payments market offer a complete service to their clients. Today, consider the following points when drawing up your guidelines for the online payment option to best suit your business.

- *What kind of goods do you sell?* If you sell expensive goods, then accepting credit card payments online is economically feasible. The overheads that these payments attract make credit cards unsuitable for small payments. Always ask yourself what costs are involved with each payment method.
- *If you sell information that can be downloaded, credit and debit cards are not feasible.* Consider micropayment options.
- *If your customer base is used to paying via cheque, you can still offer this means of payment online.* Create a form that your customers can print out and then mail to

your offices. Why not offer a freepost address at the same time as an added incentive? At all times you must ensure that customers have a trouble free means of making a payment.

- *The Internet offers any business instant access to an international market.* If your business will receive orders from abroad you must ensure that you have a payment method that takes this into account. Companies like WorldPay specialise in this kind of multi-currency payment. The Euro should also be seriously considered if your business trades in the European Union. (The Euro is looked at in more detail on Tuesday and on Saturday.)

Designing your first E-commerce enabled website

We will be looking at three business types tomorrow that will illustrate how business can make E-commerce the very centre of their trading infrastructure when they appear online. Designing an E-commerce website from scratch has a number of advantages:

- Total control can be exercised over the appearance of a website
- Shopping cart and payment systems can be integrated from the start
- Branding can be enhanced with innovative use of new technologies
- Marketing and client support can also be integrated into the website.

Summary

Overall, any business can benefit from an E-commerce enhanced Internet presence. Large or small, all businesses can take advantage of this new marketplace. The fact that this new market offers a global level playing field for business is unprecedented. Competition is no longer defined by the advertising budgets that large corporations can wield in the marketplace.

Over the next six days you will see how your business can empower itself in this new market, and thus move into the next millennium with confidence.

E-commerce case studies

Today we will look closely at three very different companies
and how they have implemented an E-commerce strategy.
We will cover corporate, medium and small businesses
where you will see how each has approached the Internet
and E-commerce – by making their presence on the Web
unique they are reaping the benefits of a well thought out
Internet strategy. In each case you will see:

- how each business approached its move to the Internet
- how they decided on the E-commerce system for them
- how they organise their delivery logistics
- how each copes with a world-wide marketplace
- how each uses the unique features of the Web to improve
  their customer relations.

Corporate business

Large corporate businesses continue to use the Web as a
new marketing channel. The wholesale move to Web based
business has yet to take place. There are, however, a number
of large companies that have developed an Internet policy,
and implemented it as part of their overall business strategy.
One such business is RS Components (rswww.com), which
launched its Internet Trading Channel in February 1998.
Part of Electrocomponents plc, it is Europe's leading
distributor of over 160,000 electronic, electrical and
mechanical components, health and safety products and
associated tools. RS UK is well known for its extensive
technical product range and its service promise: *'Order by
8 p.m. – with you tomorrow.'* The trading statistics associated
with the company are staggering:

- every 10 seconds an engineer somewhere in the world is ordering from RS
- Electrocomponents distributes to over 160 countries
- RS processes over 15,000 orders per day
- approximately 25,000 parcels are sent world-wide each day
- as of March 1999, RS UK has 110,000 products in its catalogue
- in addition to printed catalogues, RS now distributes over 1 million CD ROM catalogues each year.

The Internet Trading Channel initiative has offered RS Components a number of advantages:

- it opens a completely new channel of contact for customers
- it allows RS Components to interact with its customers

- marketing can be more accurately directed at precise customers
- advanced customer support is now possible
- it simplifies the ordering process
- it drives down costs
- it is a powerful customer retention tool
- customers can decentralise their ordering but maintain central purchasing controls.

To date the RS website has over 50,000 registered customers. Of these, over 4,000 are private individuals which is a new market for RS Components. In the website's first 12 months, over 600,000 user sessions have been recorded on the website, with over 250,000 repeat visits averaging 25 minutes. The highest order value to date has been £9,600.

RS hasn't rested on its laurels, however, and has pressed on with phase 2 of its strategy, which was launched in September of 1998. RS is renowned for its massive catalogue, and faultless next-day delivery promise world-wide. It is now providing online ordering for purchase managers to make ordering from RS even easier. It is achieving this by:

- allowing stock checks online
- offering order histories – these are maintained for 13 months, and remove the need for a customer to keep their own records, something that is consistently overlooked on low cost items
- autosaving of orders – an incomplete order is saved, and then can be added to throughout the day and finally sent for processing up to 8 p.m.

- accurate input of order information is enhanced as part numbers and descriptions are displayed together – errors from telephone ordering are eliminated, cutting down on returns
- the latest technical information is linked to individual orders which are retained for 13 months – data sheets from the 15,000 that RS has available online can then easily be called.

Overall, RS uses the Internet's unique features to enhance its business, but it also allows it to provide a more individual service to its customers, which includes:

- a personalised approach – the website recognises each customer when they return to the site
- online order and payment
- stock checking online
- multiple ordering from various cost centres
- orders can be compiled over time and sent together via the Save Order function
- powerful search engine
- delivery and dispatch enhanced via the Internet.

Medium sized business

The business that we will focus on for this example is Mathmos. Since setting up their website in March 1998, it has become one of the most distinctive E-commerce websites on the Internet today. The original lava lamp was invented in 1963 by Craven Walker. Walker's company was relaunched as Mathmos in 1991 when the current owners Cressida Granger and David Mulley took over. Since then, sales have doubled every year culminating with the

Queen's Award for Export in 1997. The Mathmos website also won the prestigious *Yell* award for the best commercial website in 1998.

The Mathmos website is distinctive in a number of areas:

- its use of graphics, colour and innovative design makes the site stand out from its competitors
- Mathmos uses a *JavaScript* based E-commerce shopping system
- the site is bi-lingual, Japanese being the other language in use – Mathmos states that the look of the Japanese language itself supports the heavy design and distinctive look of their site
- it has been designed in-house in association with the design house Kerb.

Mathmos uses the unique features of the Internet to its best advantage as it can sell its specialised goods to the widest possible audience. Its website does, however, reinforce sales from its shop in the high street. The Internet offers another facet to its retail activities as:

- Mathmos can reach a global audience with its product, something not possible through a high street retail outlet
- the Web allows direct marketing that is very effective in reaching an audience that might be interested in the Mathmos product
- feedback can be assimilated into the company's product development quickly and efficiently.

Mathmos is an excellent example of a company with a specialised product that is using the Internet as a new channel to reach its customers. Using off-the-shelf Web design packages such as *FrontPage*, Mathmos quickly developed its website with its consultants Kerb. The case of Mathmos is an example of a partnership that can be developed between a retailer and an outside design consultant. We look more closely at this important issue on Saturday as part of the Action Plan.

Small business

Finally, the business that we will look at as an example of a small business is CodeBase. CodeBase is a very small business consisting of just two people. As a start-up in 1997, Rob Young, CodeBase's founder, worked between September of 1997 and March of 1998 not really expecting to sell many of the *Java* applets that he designs. (Java applets are small pieces of computer code written for use

with the Java programming language. They allow a website that uses the Java programming language to be modified in specific ways. As you would buy peripherals for your computer like a modem or scanner to extend its capabilities, Java applets extend the capabilities of the Java programming language.)

Being surprised by the response that he received, he then worked to create the CodeBase website and E-commerce elements of his business. This went live on 13 April 1998. Recently taking on a sales and marketing manager, CodeBase provides an excellent example of a small business that has taken Internet technology and utilised this within a new business. CodeBase is a model Internet business in that:

- it exists solely on the Internet
- its product is information in the form of specialised computer programs

- its delivery mechanism is totally electronic
- its payment gathering is done completely digitally.

CodeBase uses the out-of-the-box E-commerce solution called *Shop@ssistant*. This is looked at in greater detail on Wednesday when we cover electronic shop fronts. CodeBase chose this solution for a number of reasons:

- *Shop@ssistant* is ideal for the delivery of 'hard' items such as books, CDs and software
- the electronic shop front can also be used to sell 'information' goods
- local taxes, shipping charges and VAT can be added according to the customer's location
- built-in support for the NetBanx payment system
- the shop front can be added to an existing website.

As CodeBase is completely Internet based, the method of delivery it uses to ship its goods to its clients is completely electronic. CodeBase has also implemented a unique delivery method, based on the shareware concept made popular in the early days of the personal computer. Software authors would give away their programs, asking that anyone who made use of it should pay the author a royalty. The system is open to abuse, so CodeBase uses a slightly different system.

In the past, each Java applet was e-mailed to the client. Mailing updates to the applet to all registered users then became a problem as each applet could have thousands of users. CodeBase solves the problem by bringing their clients back to its website. There they can individually download the latest version of the applet they own, unlocking it with a special electronic key.

CodeBase is also working on a means of making this transaction totally automatic. A client would be able to download the applet they need as soon as their credit card details have been verified. This method has a number of advantages:

- the merchant has little or no 'hands-on' administration
- the customer comes back to the merchant's website where further contact can be made
- buying habits can be tracked and marketing information generated
- each sale that is made acts as an advertisement for the company's products.

Overall, CodeBase has a unique position as the Internet has not only supplied the platform for a completely new business, but one that could not exist in any other medium. The Internet allows CodeBase to:

- supply their 'goods' within hours of an order being placed
- take payments instantaneously
- provide consistent support
- accurately target marketing campaigns.

Having seen the benefits of E-commerce for three different types of business, in the following chapters we turn to the nuts and bolts, starting tomorrow with a look at payment systems.

Payment systems

One of the fundamental facts that any business faces is that they must ensure that they are able to take payments from their customers with the least amount of fuss. It's no accident that retailers in the high street make sure that they offer their customers every available means of paying for the goods they have chosen. On the Internet this is no different. However, any business wishing to make the most of E-commerce and their move to a virtual marketplace must offer convenient payment methods for visitors to their virtual shop.

Of the currently available systems that you can implement, one or more should suit every kind of business. They fall into four distinct categories:

- Credit and debit card payments
- Digital cash
- Micropayments
- Smart cards.

Credit cards

A simple E-commerce site could mean that you simply include on your website a form that your customers can fill in. This would include their credit or debit card number as well as their order details. This can then be e-mailed to your server or faxed to your ordering department. You then simply check your e-mail or incoming faxes for orders. All of the current Internet browsers have built-in encryption, although this is not widely known by their users. Both

Netscape's Communicator and Microsoft's Internet Explorer allow any user to e-mail sensitive information over the Internet. You may need to educate your customers about this fact. The important security issues that you need to consider will be looked at in detail on Thursday.

A full E-commerce website would, however, process your orders completely online – the credit or debit card is verified, and the funds are transferred automatically. The SET (Secure Electronic Transfer) is a security system that stands at the heart of the major credit card companies push into E-commerce. This will also be looked at closely on Thursday when we cover security issues. For the moment, we will look at two third-party implementations that you can use to offer credit card facilities on your website.

NetBanx

This solution is an off-the-shelf service that any firm can implement as part of its E-commerce solution. This system offers a number of advantages.

1. *Portability*
   You do not need to be a NetBanx customer to use their servers to host your website. Your website can reside on any server, anywhere in the world.

2. *User-friendly verification*
   This system authorises a transaction with the least amount of fuss. Both the merchant and the customer are informed of the transaction's authorisation or rejection in seconds.

3. *Affordability*
   This system has normal merchant set-up costs. There are no hidden fees.

4. *Security*
   The problem of consumer confidence is solved as each card number that is sent for verification is given a transaction reference number. The card number itself is never revealed to the merchant.

5. *Multi-currency*
   The NetBanx system can handle transactions in over 100 different currencies.

The NetBanx solution offers the small business a means of taking credit card orders with the least amount of setting-up on their part. The NetBanx system is simply added to a company's existing website as an order payment system.

WorldPay

WorldPay Ltd operates throughout Europe, North America and Asia, and offers a complete payment system to online merchants. This system can handle single and multi-currencies, credit and debit cards, micropayments, and business-to-business transactions.

Using the established encryption techniques of public and private keys authentication, WorldPay offers not only privacy, but high security. With the additional option of digital certification when requested, this is one of the most secure systems available. WorldPay offers a number of payment solutions. One or more can be incorporated into your E-commerce division:

- *CurrencyPay*
- *LocalPay*
- Micropayments
- *BusinessPay*

CurrencyPay
This system is at the heart of the WorldPay service. Like NetBanx it offers merchants full processing of credit and debit card payments. Payments can be taken in sixteen currencies, with the customer seeing the exact price of the item they are purchasing in their own currency. WorldPay automatically updates the exchange rates on its customers' websites so the prices that are shown are always accurate based on that day's exchange rates.

LocalPay
Like *CurrencyPay*, this system allows secure transactions, but only in a single currency. Sixteen currencies are

available at present. *LocalPay* is directly linked to a number of bank processing systems. This ensure that the merchant receives the funds in the shortest possible time.

Micropayments
One area that has long stood as a barrier to smaller payments being made with credit and debit cards are the cost overheads that processing the card payment always attracts. This is solved with the micropayments system. Customers can now make payments in the smallest denomination in any of the currencies that the WorldPay system supports. Micropayments are available to anyone who has a valid credit or debit card.

BusinessPay
This is a business-to-business payment method. High value items can now be purchased securely in any of the 16 currencies that WorldPay currently supports. A master account is setup, and then any number of trading accounts. A business can then sell to distributors. A credit limit is set for each customer that uses the master account. They each have their own trading account which is used for the transfer of funds each time a purchase is made.

Digital cash

Digital cash stands between credit card payments and smart card technology. Often used as a generic term to describe all forms of electronic money, there are a number of specific systems available, or in development, that allow a customer to buy goods online.

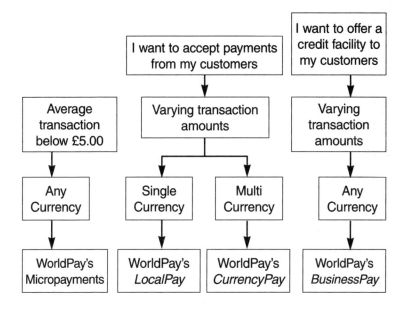

One such system is being pioneered by Barclays Bank in the UK. Their *BarclayCoin* system is based on a US system developed by CyberCash Inc. This system allows payments to be accepted that are usually too small to allow a credit card to be used, due to the high overhead costs that these cards attract. Payments as low as 25p can be made and up to a maximum of £10.00. Low cost items such as utility programmes, clip art and sound files can be purchased with this system. The system operates with two types of software.

- *BarclayCoin* Wallet
- Cash Register

BarclayCoin Wallet
A customer must first create a personal Wallet to keep their

electronic money in. When this is done they use their existing credit card to transfer funds to this Wallet, which are then turned into *BarclayCoin* funds. This process is known as binding your card. The Wallet is then ready to use online to make purchases. The Wallet has a number of unique features:

- it is kept on your own PC, and not a remote server
- it transfers funds from VISA, Mastercard, Switch
- a maximum of £40.00 can be stored in a Wallet
- funds can be transferred back to your credit or debit card from the Wallet at any time – there is no fund transfer fee for this service
- it has a complete transaction log that acts as electronic receipts.

Barclays Bank provides the retailer with all the software they need to attach to their website to take advantage of *BarclayCoin*. All merchants at the moment need to have an agreement with Barclays Merchant Services to use this system, and presently only UK based businesses can use the service. Once setup, they can then offer means for customers to buy low cost items - usually delivered digitally over the Internet - simply.

Cash Register
The Cash Register handles the entire transaction, from the request from the customer for the goods, to the actual transfer of the items to the customer's PC, and then the transfer of funds from the customer's Wallet to the merchant's account. The Cash Register also keeps a transaction history, and a running total of the goods sold.

Micropayments

Until recently E-commerce was limited to high value items.
There is, however, an emerging marketplace that could
fundamentally change the way that business is done on the
Internet. Micropayment systems offer a means of making
small payments for information. Fractions of a penny or
cent can be used to buy a news item from an online
newspaper, a stock market quote, tomorrow's weather
forecast, or to have a new cartoon delivered to your PC
each morning.

Information based businesses are looking for ways in
which they can sell their goods over the Internet as this
allows them to bypass the high costs of packaging and
shipping the items to customers. Low cost items have
always suffered due to the inadequate payment systems

that are available, most notably credit and debit cards. The high overhead cost of processing the transactions has barred their use in the microcommerce marketplace. Today we will look at one such micropayment system: *MilliCent*, based in the USA.

MilliCent

This payment system supports transactions valued between one tenth of a cent and $5.00. The *MilliCent* system uses brokers and what is called *scrip*. The broker takes care of all the transactions that use as the method of payment, and this can be in any currency. Micropayments are therefore ideal to:

• sell low cost items over the Internet
• collect subscription fees from customers
• allocate loyalty points
• sell software updates
• prioritise access
• charge internal costs centres.

How the *MilliCent* system works

The system is comprised of three components:

• the *MilliCent Wallet*
• the *MilliCent Vendor Service*
• the *MilliCent Broker Service.*

Instead of using a credit card to make a payment, *MilliCent* uses electronic tokens called *scrip*. This is like loose change. Customers buy scrip using a credit or debit card from an authorised broker. This can then be exchanged for content as they visit various websites.

MilliCent Wallet

The Wallet is held on the customer's PC and is used to buy, hold and spend the *MilliCent* scrip. The Wallet can be set up to automatically pay for content as it is brought on the Internet, up to a set limit.

MilliCent Vendor Service

This is the server side of the system and is where a content provider or merchant's website will take and process orders for content. The *Vendor Service* validates scrip to make sure that it hasn't been spent before and that there is adequate scrip to make the purchase.

MilliCent Broker Service

This last component is also based on the merchant's server and is where money is converted into scrip. To keep costs to a minimum, the system does not use strong encryption. As the amounts of money are so small, it is felt that any overhead cost in forging scrip makes counterfeiting uneconomical.

MilliCent security

As this micropayment system reduces transaction costs so is also provides a number of security features.

- As scrip is used for small purchases, customers treat it as they would loose change.
- No receipt is issued for the goods sold. However, if they don't arrive, the Replay button can be used. You will learn more about this feature later in this section.
- Encryption is used to validate scrip, stopping it from being stolen or counterfeited.

- Scrip is vendor specific, so double-spending is eliminated.
- Broker and vendor fraud is discouraged as the transaction amounts are so small.

Smart cards

Smart cards look, to all intents and purposes, just like traditional credit cards. They differ in that they have a microchip embedded in their surface that can be used to store a wide range of information about the holder of the card, or be used as a means of carrying electronic cash. They offer the advantages of paying by cash, but with the convenience of paying by card.

Customers can load their card with cash and then use this to pay for goods in a merchant's retail outlet, or on the merchant's w ebsite. Card readers are available for retail outlets as well as an attachment for PCs. This convenience gives a great advantage to smart cards as they can be used in the physical world as well as on the Internet.

There are two types of smart card:

Disposable
These cards have a value permanently attached to them. They work just as today's phonecards do. They have no protection against loss. Anyone can use a disposable smart card.

Reloadable
These cards have more memory and can carry vastly more information than disposable cards, and have high levels of

security. These will be looked at in more detail on Thursday. These cards are able to be reloaded with digital cash, which can then be spent in retail outlets, or over the Internet.

The most mature of the smart card technologies that is being used in the electronic cash market is *Mondex*. The *Mondex* smart card has a number of unique features.

For the customer:

- it can be loaded with cash from a wide variety of locations – public payphone, at home via a phone, and high street ATM machines
- it makes cash more secure – if you lose banknotes or coins, they are lost permanently; if a *Mondex* card is lost it cannot be used by anyone else as it is electronically locked
- with the aid of a *Mondex* card reader, the amount of cash left on the card can be easily read
- you always know where the money has gone as all cards keep a transaction log.
- there is no need to worry about change – *Mondex* cards always present the exact amount of cash that is needed.

For the retailer:

- where credit and debit cards need authorisation, smart cards don't as the cash is already held on the card
- transactions are quicker – as exact amounts are paid, merchants don't have to keep large amounts of cash on their premises
- it provides lower overheads
- it allows for fraud control.

The Euro

As of 1st January 1999, the Euro has become a legal currency within 11 countries of the EU. All of the major payment providers will be supporting this currency, as will UK banks. Merchant Services from the UK banks that support services such as NetBanx and WorldPay will also allow the websites that they process online transactions for to action payments in euros. The Euro will be treated like a foreign currency and converted to appropriate currencies when this is needed.

However, any business that is trading on the Internet from the UK must take into consideration the effects that this currency will have on their business when setting prices for their goods and services, as the advent of the Euro will mean:

- Cheaper transaction costs will be enjoyed by all business trading within the Euro Zone.
- Elimination of exchange rates within the Euro Zone. If products are bought in euros, the exchange rate risk between sterling and euros will transfer to the purchaser. This could have adverse effects on a company's income.
- Exporters may need to begin to quote in euros when trading with their partners.
- If your company operates business-to-business, you may be asked to deal in euros if you are part of a supply chain.
- Retailers with an online presence may want to show prices on their websites not only in their existing currency but converted to euros as well.

Overall, as the Internet does not recognise national borders and offers every business a level and international market to trade in, all UK based business will have to think carefully about how they will handle the Euro. On Saturday we will look closer at this point, and about how business can implement a strategy to handle the Euro, when we consider global markets.

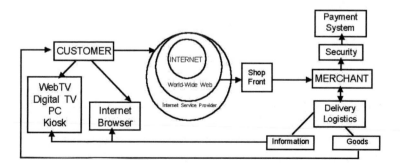

Electronic payment systems summary flow chart

Electronic shop fronts

Today we will look closely at a variety of shop fronts and E-commerce software packages that allow a company of any size to build a successful electronic business. Just as a retail chain has shops and stores that allow it to sell its goods to customers, on the Internet a business must still design and build a website that is attractive but above all functional, i.e. one that doesn't stand in a customer's way when they wish to make a purchase. The shop fronts that we look at today cover all business types and sizes.

Microsoft *Site Server*, Enterprise Edition

Microsoft's E-commerce solution is a complete set of hardware and software tools that allows any medium to large business to build an effective E-commerce website.

The Enterprise Edition of Microsoft's *Site Server* includes Commerce Server, the new name for Microsoft's Merchant Server which was introduced in 1996. Microsoft now offer complete integration with its tools as they now support:

- Microsoft Internet Explorer 4
- Windows NT
- The Microsoft Wallet

Overall Microsoft's products address a number of fundamental areas:

- cost of set up which is tailored to the individual company's needs
- *Site Server Commerce 3.0* includes Wizards and tools for fast development of a website
- commerce Interchange Pipeline simplifies working with EDI
- third parties can develop 'snap-ins', small pieces of custom written computer code to handle any kind of payment method
- payment methods can be used with Microsoft's Wallet technology
- Windows NT security is integrated with the Site Server
- advertising with promotions, buy-now and cross-sell targeting
- fully scalable.

The *Site Server Commerce* package provides two tools: the *Site Foundation Wizard*, and the *Store Builder Wizard*. The *Site Foundation Wizard* allows the creation of the BackOffice areas of your site. This sets up the database connections you will use, and supports ODBC and SQL database formats that are used when a company is offering some of its data over the Internet.

Using the *Site Server Commerce* package allows a flexible means of organising a business' processes. *Site Server Commerce* is sold with 14 predefined states. You can delete stages, or add your own, either created yourself, or bought from a third party. The predefined stages are:

• product information	• merchant information
• shopper information	• order initialisation
• order check	• item price
• item price adjustment	• order price adjustment
• subtotal	• handling
• shipping	• total
• tax	• inventory adjustment

If your primary trade is business-to-business selling, Microsoft's solution can also provide support:

- cost centres can replace credit card payments
- requisition approval can be added to the above stages in your order processing pipeline

- multiple catalogues can be combined
- submission formats can be more flexible, e.g. mail or fax
- backend operations can be modified to trigger orders from suppliers.

Summary
Microsoft's *Site Server* Commerce Edition also offers businesses a number of features that they can build into their E-commerce enabled website:

- optimisation for Windows NT operating system
- targeted online advertising
- personalised promotions
- secure order taking
- scalable systems
- integration with existing accounting, inventory, and EDI systems
- customer analysis.

IBM *HomePage Creator* and *Net.Commerce*

IBM offers a number of different services and products for businesses of any size that would like to buy an off-the-shelf E-commerce solution. Today we will look at IBM's *HomePage Creator* service which is aimed at the small business user, and IBM's *Net.Commerce* in its START configuration.

HomePage Creator

Like many of the other packages that are available, this system allows the creation of an E-commerce enabled website with the use of templates and a hosting service from IBM itself. *HomePage Creator* has a number of features that make it ideal for the small business, or a new business setting up on the Internet for the first time.

- You can use your existing Internet browser and the Java based tools that IBM provide to create your website's page, or upload pages that you have created with another package.
- A gallery of graphics is available to use on your website, or upload your own.
- No programming knowledge of HTML or FTP is needed – your Web pages are created online via the IBM website.
- There are over 150 different themed templates to choose from.
- Your website is hosted on secure IBM servers (IBM RS/6000).
- You are allocated a custom site name.
- The package includes shopping cart, product catalogue and credit card processing.
- Through a link with *Submit It!* your website will be registered with 20 of the most popular search engines.
- It is cost effective. At the time of writing, *HomePage Creator* costs £15 per month plus VAT, plus £15 set up fee for the Bronze service. For £15 your site can have up to 12 items, increasing to a maximum of 500 items for £120 per month, plus £90 set up fee with the Platinum service.
- You can expand your website as you need to – *HomePage Creator* expands with your business.
- You have the opportunity to create a site in a variety of languages.
- Online customer payments are handled by NetBanx.

Net.Commerce

IBM also offers E-commerce solutions for SMEs and large corporations through its Net.Commerce services. The service comes in two flavours with each offering their own unique set of applications to match every business type and need. *Net.Commerce* can:

- pinpoint the time and location of customer orders
- build customer profiles
- integrate with your existing technology such as inventory, shipping and tax information
- deliver real-time data
- track customer preferences and actions
- target promotions, time-limited offers, and special messages to specific customer groups
- improve customer retention and increase sales
- link to IBM's DB2 database, and any other ODBC standard databases
- support Open Buying on the Internet (OBI) for business-to-business transactions.

Net.Commerce START

For the SME that wants to set up on the Internet quickly, START offers a shop front wizard, secure payment systems, and support for the Domino Go Web server. Pricing starts at £3,200 for the entry level package. *Net.Commerce* START has a number of features that are available out-of-the-box:

- runs on Windows NT 4.0
- uses familiar browser interface and wizards to create your online site
- predefined catalogue templates

- shopping cart, order form, check-out and customer registration
- can be configured for business-to-customer, or business-to-business use
- payment server that is SET (Secure Electronic Transactions) supported
- Year 2000 ready.

Shop@ssistant

Outside of the large corporations that we have looked at today, smaller companies have moved into the shop front creation market with a number of packages designed to get your business online as quickly and as cost effectively as possible. CodeBase, who we looked at as a case study on Monday, uses this system. *Shop@ssistant* from the Floyd Consultancy (www.floyd.co.uk) offers the small business two versions of their package: *Classic* and *Lite*.

Shop@ssistant Classic

Classic offers any business a complete solution, but will particularly appeal to SMEs who have inventory that they would like to put into an online shop front. *Shop@ssistant* offers a complete out-of-the-box solution with the following benefits:

- low cost – *Shop@ssistant* costs £199 (excl VAT)
- it integrates into an existing website
- your website can be hosted by any ISP (Internet Service Provider)
- the system runs on your customer's browser so is particularly fast
- it requires no server-side scripts so reducing the complexity of the site
- secure transactions are assured via a recognised merchant service such as NetBanx
- alternative payment options are supported such as COD, cheques or bank transfers
- VAT calculations are included
- carriage charges can be calculated based on weight, volume, destination zone or carrier
- facilities to make discounts and include special offers are available
- there is no service charge or monthly subscription fee
- a multi-currency version is available (£299)
- it comes completely independent of Web design tools.

Shop@ssistant Lite

Appreciating even the low price point that their Classic version offered, the Floyd Consultancy have developed an even more compact and cost effective version of their product. *Shop@ssistant Lite* offers:

- a low price of £49.99
- only one page of products available
- Web pages which are built automatically and uploaded to your server
- payment systems as comprehensive as the *Classic* version
- delivery costs which are simplified into four zones
- easy up-grade path to the *Classic* version.

Summary

A business selling a service to its clients, or a business with thousands of items on its catalogue, can set up a shop front on the Internet with *Shop@ssistant*. Larger businesses that need more integration with BackOffice and legacy systems may find this system lacking in some areas. However, for a retail based business, *Shop@ssistant* offers:

- complete integration with payment systems
- customisable pages which allow your website to be designed to your exact requirements
- carriage and VAT charges which can be calculated automatically
- a complete out-of-the-box solution
- a facility not limited to the seller's ISP
- all programming and Web code hidden from the user.

Security

Any company that wishes to trade on the Internet must provide adequate levels of security for itself, as well as for its clients and customers. The Internet can provide higher levels of customer security than the traditional retail outlets in the high street. Nonetheless, it is still a matter of great concern to the vast majority of would be online consumers. Today we will look at how a business that is contemplating an E-commerce move to the Internet, or one that already has a presence, can enhance its security features to enable it to increase its own confidence and, as a consequence, extend that security confidence to its customers.

We will look closely at:

- the means of ensuring security when payments are being made
- the available forms of encryption that can be employed on your website
- how you can protect your own website from attack from outside of your organisation if you are – or are planning to – host your own website on your own server.

Secure transactions

To ensure security for your business and your customers you need:

- privacy
- to be able to clearly identify all parties in a transaction

- to have complete integrity in that the information sent should not be altered in any way
- confidentiality – once the transaction has taken place, it should be erased from the system.

Encryption

The information that your customers and clients will be sending to your companies website needs to be treated with the utmost confidence. Personal information, as well as credit and debit card numbers, must be secure at all times. This can be achieved with encryption. With a good system in place, your customers can feel secure that the information they are giving will not be intercepted en route to your website, and that any information sent is not modified in any way. The most widely used and secure method of encryption today is called Public-Key Encryption.

Public-Key encryption

The British Government has proposed to set up an organisation to control Public-Keys and in 1996 announced support for key escrow which would mean that every private key used by business would be deposited with a Trusted Third Party in an attempt to combat crime. The Government faced a dilemma in that it wished to monitor transactions – giving the law enforcement community access to encryption keys of criminals – without endangering free trade.

In 1997 the Government released proposals to promote key escrow in the DTI's consultation paper 'Licensing of Trusted Third Parties for the Provision of Encryption Services.' (www.dti.gov.uk/pubs). However, on 26 May 1999 the Government abandoned these proposals as unworkable, reacting to industry's lobbying that such legislation would in fact hinder E-commerce on the Internet.

The Electronic Commerce Bill, will, however, make it an offence to not decrypt material when requested to do so by the security authorities, or provide the necessary keys to decrypt files on request, or hide the location of these keys. These new powers will be introduced with the Police and Criminal Evidence Act. Now we will look at two other security systems that are in place today: SSL and SET.

SSL (Secure Socket Layer)

Netscape Communications, the creators of Navigator (the world's first graphical Internet browser), developed SSL as a solution to the security problems associated with transferring information over the Internet. SSL is also supported by Microsoft in its Internet Explorer browser. SSL allows a standard browser to be used to transmit and receive information securely. SSL is convenient for a number of reasons:

- it is integrated into the browser – no additional software is needed
- the encryption key is different each time the browser is used, adding to its security
- information is automatically encrypted on transmission, and decrypted on reception
- it uses 40-bit long keys that are hard to break
- SSL is application independent.

How does it work?
When a customer visits your website their Internet browser contacts your server and asks for the pages that they want to see. This information is sent and then received through what are called 'sockets'. The problem with this situation is that the data that is sent is not encrypted, and can be freely read and copied by anyone. If the data your customer is sending includes a credit card number, for instance, this could be a major security risk.

SSL solves this problem of an open connection by encrypting the data as it passes to and from the browser and the server. The strength of SSL is based on the difficulty that anyone would have if they wanted to decrypt the information. At the moment, 40-bit long encryption is used which is secure enough for financial transactions, although longer keys will eventually come into use. The general rule is that the longer the key is, the harder it is to crack; but more computing power is required to both generate the key and decrypt the message on receipt.

SET (Secure Electronic Transfer)

Announced in February 1996 by VISA and MasterCard, this encryption system has been gaining ground since its introduction as it is specific to credit card transactions over the Internet. Again the system uses public-key cryptography to secure the transactions. SET aims to:

- give full confidentiality for all payments
- ensure that all transmitted data is not compromised in any way
- authenticate the card holder
- authenticate the merchant and their bankers
- provide interoperability – the SET standard can be used on a wide variety of hardware and software platforms.

How does it work?
As a means of illustrating how SET comes into use in a typical transaction on the Internet, we will look at a hypothetical transaction which would be typical in today's E-commerce environment.

1 The merchant will have set up their website, and E-commerce enabled the site with easy 'buy now' buttons near each of the goods or services that are on offer.

2 A customer that visits the merchant's site selects the items that they would like to buy. This could be via an electronic shopping basket.

3 The customer completes the order form that will contain their delivery details.

4 The card holder now selects the method of payment that they would like to use. This is where SET begins to enter the transaction process.

5 The completed order is then sent to the merchant's server where it is processed. SET will use the card holder's digital signature and attach this to the payment as it is processed. This proves that this order came from that card holder and no one else.

6 The merchant then requests payment from the issuer of the card holder. SET is used to encrypt this request. A merchant must have a digital certificate that represents the merchant's relationship to his bank. This relationship also handles the public-key encryption that is used to secure the transaction, and lastly the credit card information is encoded with a digital signature that proves the identity of the card holder.

7 The goods or services are shipped to the customer.

SET is fast becoming a standard for electronic payments on the Internet. One of its major strengths for the consumer is that the credit card numbers of customers are never known to the merchant as this information is encrypted and only decrypted by the card's issuing bank when a payment is presented for authentication and authorisation by the merchant.

Firewalls

As the stock of a retail outlet is protected by plate glass, steel shutters and electronic security systems, so any business that has its systems connected to the Internet must ensure that only those individuals and organisations that it has authorised can access their website on their servers.

A firewall is a separate computer system that acts as a gateway or a filter that all transactions must pass through. Very much like a toll booth on a bridge, a company can configure the firewall to allow any specific information through and reject all other types. Large companies are more likely to have Intranets and therefore require firewall protection. However, even the smallest company that wishes to trade on the Internet must address its security issues.

A small business will probably buy its E-commerce systems, which will include the Internet connection itself, from a third party. Customers wishing to make payments for goods or services should be offered the highest possible security when making these payments.

Packet Filtering Firewall

As its name suggests, this type of firewall filters packets of information as they enter your business systems. You can set up this type of firewall, for instance, to allow through only e-mail from certain sources, or data from chosen websites. All other data that tries to enter your server will be rejected. However, this type of firewall suffers from a number of disadvantages:

- it is difficult to decide which types of data to allow through the firewall
- once the system is set up it is inflexible
- if the system is breached, the whole network can come under attack.

The alternative to a simple packet filtering firewall is the proxy server.

Proxy Server Firewalls

This kind of firewall is situated between the Internet and a company's internal network, as with the packet filtering firewall. However, as a packet filtering firewall is usually a hardware gateway attached to a company's router, a proxy firewall exists as a software application. Incoming traffic first contacts this proxy software which then connects the traffic to the appropriate area of the company's website. Proxy firewalls offer a number of advantages:

- anonymity – all internal system names are known only to the proxy
- authentication – all traffic can be logged before it reaches its destination
- they manage network functions and create audit trails based on date, time, byte count and IP address of all incoming traffic
- access can be controlled based on browser type, domain name etc.

Proxy firewalls also have some disadvantages:

- access is a two-step process
- poor protection against viruses
- bottlenecks can form in the traffic accessing the proxy firewall.

When implementing a firewall policy a company must consider:

- the overall security policy of the company – the firewall must not be undermined by lax security in other areas of the company
- how much auditing is to be carried out on the firewall
- the risk level at which the firewall is set up to withhold
- who is to maintain the firewall.

Lastly don't forget that a firewall cannot protect against:

- inside intrusion
- attack from areas that are not protected via the firewall itself
- virus attack.

Summary

Security on the Internet is an ongoing contentious issue that has held back the development of E-commerce, and prevented consumers from making purchases online. Today, there are security features such as SSL and SET that offer protection to the consumer when shopping online, and should allow the rapid development of E-commerce over the next few years.

As customer confidence grows, so security issues will take a back seat allowing companies to concentrate on the business of selling their goods and services. Once your company has put in place the technology that will allow secure access to your own Intranet for instance, and set up the company's website to incorporate the latest security features for payments, you can then move your energies away from these issues and concentrate on developing the next stage in the retailing process: order fulfilment. We cover this subject tomorrow.

Logistics

Today we will be looking closely at one of the
fundamentally important aspects of any business, the
delivery of goods and services to their customers. With the
advent of the Internet, and E-commerce, many companies
are finding that they must suddenly deliver their products
to a global market. This can have its own problems, but can
be handled with an effective logistics policy.

Logistics – the movement of goods within a market – has been
transformed over the past few years. In 1980, for instance, the
USA spent 10.8% of its GDP on inventory. By 1995 that figure
had dropped to just 4.3%. This startling reduction is a clear
indication that efficiency improvements in logistics have taken
place. However, the USA still spent $700 billion in 1996 on
inventory, and its transportation.

(Source: *Blueprint to the Digital Economy*. McGraw Hill, 1998.)

Businesses based on the E-commerce model fall into two categories: those that deliver goods to their customers through the traditional means of transportation, and use the Internet as a shop front; and those that use the Internet to not only attract their customers but also deliver their product (which is often information based) over the Internet. We will look first at the logistics that revolve around the delivery of physical goods to customers, and how the Internet, and your E-commerce presence, can be used to enhance your business.

Physical goods

Most E-commerce businesses will have goods to sell. The delivery of those goods is paramount to the success of any business. When the move to the Internet is made, this urgency becomes more apparent as customers do not wish to wait unduly for the goods they have chosen and paid for. An E-commerce business must therefore ensure that it:

- has the required inventory to supply the goods displayed on its Web site
- has an effective and efficient delivery mechanism in place, with a reliable carrier
- tracks each order with enough detail to correct any mistakes that have been made
- has an effective returns policy.

Case Study

FedEx
One business that has used the art of logistics to create a global business is Federal Express. Fred Smith founded

FedEx as a shipping company in 1973. FedEx offered its clients a means of enhancing their businesses by providing a fast and efficient delivery service.

The company's growth has been phenomenal. In 1997, FedEx were shipping three million parcels per day, in 212 countries, relying on 600 planes, 40,000 trucks and vans, a staff of 140,000, with revenues reaching $11.5 billion.

(Source: *Blueprint to the Digital Economy*. McGraw Hill, 1998.)

FedEx have found that their investment in the Internet (including its integration within their own business) can also be extended to their clients, as an effective logistical policy allows:

* reduced costs
* consolidation of information – customer trends can be spotted and exploited early
* forward planning
* customer care – as the Internet is now used to bring the customer into the delivery process, a rapport can be built that allows a mutual confidence to grow.

The example of FedEx clearly shows that an effective logistics policy is paramount. Any E-commerce based business can take advantage of the services that are offered by companies like FedEx. An important step further, however, is learning from their experience, and the way that information technology, with special reference to the Internet, can transform a company's delivery policy.

Outsourcing

Companies like FedEx offer the ultimate in outsourcing.
Many smaller companies that enter a global market cannot
hope to maintain their own distribution network.
Outsourcing the distribution element of an E-commerce
based business has many advantages:

- Reduced costs – maintaining a fleet of delivery trucks in
  your own country is expensive; on a global scale this is
  not feasible
- Customer response – orders can be fulfilled faster as the
  logistics of placing that order in your customer's hands
  have been outsourced to a specialised carrier
- Pricing – a manufacturer can price their goods for a
  global market as delivery costs are known
- Cost effective for small companies.

Information delivery

At its most fundamental level the Internet is an information
provider, but one that is unlike any other devised so far. It
has one profound advantage over other information
delivery systems such as books and magazines, radio and
TV: the Internet is interactive. We have already looked at
how a manufacturer can use the Internet to sell their goods
to a global market. In this section we will consider how
businesses that sell information can take advantage of the
unique features of the Internet. For the information
provider the Internet offers:

- a global market for their product
- a means of targeting their product to specialised
  customer bases

- a customisable product
- a means of enhancing an existing product with extra added value
- a means of attracting new customers that were previously unattainable.

As a focus for this section we will look at the publishing industry, one that has been profoundly affected over the past few years as the Internet has grown in importance. The magazine publisher in particular has been offered the chance to redefine itself thanks to this new delivery system.

If your business provides information to a customer base, the Internet can be used both to sell that product more effectively and deliver that product more efficiently and at much lower costs. As we saw on Monday, there are businesses that exist totally on the Internet. Their product is created electronically, delivered electronically, with support, payments, and updates all handled on the Internet.

As an example of how the Internet can be used to enhance the business whose product is information based, we will consider a fictitious publisher of a specialised newsletter. How can this business use the Internet to sell information that has previously been printed and sold to customers via the traditional mail routes?

A newsletter can be enhanced by moving it to the Internet for a number of reasons.

1 The publisher can increase its profit margin as the costs of distributing the newsletter are almost zero.

2 The publisher can better target their audience and therefore offer their advertisers a more focused database of readers to sell to.

3 New content can be added that is impossible with the printed version of the newsletter – multimedia content can be used to enhance a particular issue.

4 Thus, value can be added to the online version of the newsletter so attracting existing and new readers to the online version's Web site. This then has the knock-on effect of enhancing the available advertising base that the newsletter can sell to.

5 A much wider audience can be catered for. As the Net is global, and delivery costs are almost nil, the publisher can create a product for a much more geographically diverse audience. Where the cost of producing a version of the newsletter for each audience, and then

delivering this, were prohibitively expensive, these
constraints have been wiped out by the Internet.

Publishing is of course the tip of the iceberg in the field of
information delivery. Services such as financial products,
software and other digital products can also be delivered
over the Internet. Banking has fundamentally changed over
the past few years, with an ever-increasing number of
services now available to online consumers.

Software is the perfect product for delivery over the
Internet. However, there are still a number of constraints
that the existing Internet has that must be considered if
your business wants to move to a digital product. Services
can be sold over the Net with few constraints. The software
provider can also offer this service to its clients, as can the
music publisher. In the next few years music may be solely
bought over the Internet. However, in all these businesses
where a digital product is being sold to an ever increasing
global customer base, any business must consider:

- The Internet still suffers from lack of bandwidth. Text and sound can be delivered with acceptable speed to a customer, and a payment gathered. However, other digital media such as video is still not technically possible at acceptable speeds and quality.
- The Net offers a global market. Smaller companies may find it difficult to modify their product for this increasingly diverse market, if their product is of universal appeal. Conversely, specialised markets can thrive on the Net as it offers a means of reaching these diverse markets that were previously unreachable.
- Where an audience was previously captive, today readerships have more power to decide what content they read, and from whom. The Net offers the consumer a means of deciding what they would like to see, and buy, without the traditional filters of editors. Any information based business must ensure that they are offering content that is attractive to this audience.

Electronic Data Interchange

Finally today we will look briefly at EDI. At the moment Electronic Data Interchange is operated by large businesses as the costs involved in setting up and maintaining the system make it prohibitively expensive for smaller businesses. However, with the advent of the Internet, this is slowly changing as more businesses embrace this system. We look at EDI here as it offers a means that any business can use – when costs are suitably reduced – to enhance the logistical element of a business.

Simply put, EDI is a means of transferring data to and from companies, via computer, using a standard set of formats.

Initially used by the transportation industry, it is now in wide use in the manufacturing sector, in businesses as diverse as pharmaceuticals and banking. These documents can be purchase orders, bills of exchange or invoices. Any paper based administration tasks can be handled by EDI. Large supermarket chains for instance use EDI to order from their wide range of suppliers.

When thinking about your logistical plans for your E-commerce business, EDI may be a system that will need to be set up if you are going to be dealing with larger companies that you will be supplying. If your customer base is mainly consumers you will probably not need to take EDI on board. If your business does, however, need to set this system up, EDI has a number of advantages.

Advantages

- reduced administration costs
- elimination of errors
- reduced processing time
- reduces inventory, and make just-in-time inventory management a reality
- a complete audit trail is generated – this information is vital to improve the overall systems performance

EDI does, however, have its downside.

Disadvantages

- high set up costs
- the system is not designed for merchant-consumer contact
- EDI is very structured which makes it inflexible, and difficult to modify once it is set up

- EDI is a specialised function for the procurement of goods or services – accounting and inventory systems are not included in the overall system which can result in discrepancies
- partners in an EDI system enter into a closed system that is difficult to break into for new suppliers; the Internet is, however, changing this situation.

Summary

When setting up the logistical organisation of your business think carefully about the following points.

- Who do you sell to? Consumers or other businesses?
- How can you deliver your goods or services to your customers in the shortest time?
- Where are your customers? What are the costs involved in delivering goods or services to a global market?
- Can you track your orders, and answer queries about them?

Essential information and Action Plan

Today we will cover all the major issues that have an impact on a business that is about to move into an electronic environment. Just as taxation laws, consumer protection and customs duty apply to any business that is operating in the physical world, so these areas also need to be addressed when a business either sets up online for the first time or when an existing business moves some or all of its organisation to an E-commerce environment.

The Single European Currency

The Euro is not just an issue for the organisations based in the 11 countries of the Euro Zone. Since it will be the currency of some 300 million consumers and approximately 20 percent of the global economy, the Euro is going to affect business around the world. Given the timetable to which we must all work, Microsoft understands that there is a real need for urgency in addressing it now.

(Source: Bill Gates, Chairman & CEO, Microsoft Corporation)

Although the UK did not join the other members of the EC on the launch of the Euro in January 1999, business still needs to take steps to handle this new currency. Businesses that trade in the high street or business-to-business must take steps to implement a Euro strategy. The Euro can:

- be seen as an additional currency and dealt with in the same way as any foreign currency currently is
- be used as a guiding currency for markets within the EU

- be ignored – businesses would have to request that all monies deposited are converted to their national currency.

The Euro can, however, been seen in a very different light. Those businesses that have moved, or are planning a move, to the Internet can take advantage of this new currency and the convergence that it brings to the vast European markets that the EU consists of. Every business must ask themselves:

- Will the Euro open new markets?
- Will your suppliers be moving to the Euro?
- Will your business have a need to seek financing in Euros?

The Euro will also bring with it a number of unique circumstances that many businesses have not had to face before.

Cheaper transaction costs

Countries adopting the Euro will be able to trade with each other and enjoy almost zero transaction costs as no currency conversion is needed. Businesses in the UK that trade with those countries within the Euro Zone need to consider this fact very carefully.

Stable exchange rates

The single currency will remove exchange rates. Therefore, UK based businesses buying from suppliers in the Euro Zone will have the exchange rate risk transferred to them.

Transparent price difference

Businesses that currently charge different prices in different countries will have these price differentials brought into sharp focus. The comparison of price will become much easier. This should increase competition, but also may affect the profitability of a business as it realigns its prices to compete with those in the Euro Zone.

Internet based businesses, or businesses that have a digital channel, can use this part of their businesses to help them implement the Euro when it arrives. Every business must:

- think about the banking products that they use now – how will they be affected by the Euro?
- consider how they will be implementing the Euro – will they be making and/or receiving payments in Euros?
- assess if they need a Euro account now
- research in detail the cost involved in moving the Euro within their financial structure
- weigh up their exposure to exchange rate risk.

Business that has adopted E-commerce has a number of advantages. For example, WorldPay, one of the leading payment clearing services in the Internet that we looked at in detail on Tuesday, is implementing its own Euro strategy in response to its customer demands.

Taxation

When dealing with taxation on the Internet, a business can look to its position at the moment for a guide. The taxes that the government collect presently will apply equally to organisations operating in an online environment. What is hoped, however, is that the unique nature of the Internet doesn't spawn any new taxation, either for business or consumers.

At the moment, to all intents and purposes, the USA sets policy in this area. At a recent World Trade Organisation meeting in Geneva, President Clinton stated, 'We cannot allow discriminatory barriers to stunt the development of the most promising new economic opportunity in decades.' This sweeping statement was eventually modified and it was decided that the US government would press for 'permanently duty-free Internet.'

In Europe it is very unlikely that any of the member states would turn their backs on this lucrative taxation opportunity as a vast majority of government collected taxes are earned from consumers. At the present time EU taxation laws have the following principal effects:

- all physical goods traded over the Internet are subject to VAT at the rate of the country of origin

- goods bought from outside of the EU have VAT added at the place of despatch – in the UK, this is customs duty payable when the goods are delivered
- invisible goods and services (which includes the sale of software over the Internet) are taxed with what Customs and Excise call the 'reverse charge procedure' – VAT is applied at the buyer's side and not the seller's side.

In October 1998, Barbara Roche MP published *Net Benefit: The Electronic Commerce Agenda for the UK*. In this document Mrs Roche stated on taxation that, 'The UK Government is increasingly taking advantage of electronic methods of communication, information processing and payment in its relation with UK taxpayers. The UK Government believes the following broad principles should apply to the taxation of electronic commerce:

- *Neutrality.* Taxation should seek to be technology neutral so that no particular form of commerce is advantaged or disadvantaged.
- *Certainty and transparency.* Rules should be clear and simple so that businesses can anticipate, so far as possible, the tax consequences of the transaction they enter into.
- *Effectiveness.* Tax rules should not result in double taxation or unintentional nontaxation. Risks of increased evasion or avoidance should be kept to a minimum.
- *Efficiency.* The compliance costs of business and the administration costs of government should be kept to the minimum compatible with effective tax administration. Measures to counter evasion or avoidance should be proportionate to the risks which they seek to address.'

In conclusion, Mrs Roche states in her paper, 'At this stage there is no need for major changes to existing tax rules, or for the introduction of new taxes.'

At the present time the UK tax position regarding the sale of goods and services over the Internet can be summarised thus:

- Taxation (VAT) is charged in the country of consumption.
- Goods and services supplied electronically will be treated as services and are free of import duty, but remain liable for VAT.

Legal issues

Copyright and intellectual property rights

What is copyright?

Copyright gives rights to the creators of certain kinds of material to control the various ways in which their material may be exploited.   (Source: The Patent Office)

Today more than ever the creators of any material that is copyrightable have to consider the legal and enforceable elements of material that may find its way onto the Internet. In this section we will look at what is copyrightable, what intellectual property is, and how it can be protected when it is used online.

Material that can be copyrighted comprises:

- original works of literature, music recordings, artistic works, films and broadcasts (which includes cable and satellite)
- computer programs which are protected as if they were literary works
- databases.

Material that cannot be copyrighted comprises:

- names
- ideas
- industrial articles e.g., the drawings for an article can be copyrighted, but the item that results from those drawings cannot be copyrighted.

The Internet

Under UK law, any material that holds a copyright in the physical world also holds copyright when on the Internet. If material resides on a Web server, and is copied to another location without the permission of the copyright holder, this constitutes an infringement of the owner's copyright.

Businesses should also note that scanning, photocopying and digitising any copyrighted work, which is then disseminated in any way without the express permission of the copyright holder, also constitutes a copyright infringement.

Further information is available from:

The British Copyright Council
Copyright House
29-33 Berners Street
London W1P 4AA

Tel: 01986-788122.   Fax: 01986-78847.

E-mail: copyright@bcc2.demon.co.uk

Contracts

Contracts, especially between businesses but also between suppliers and their customers, have moved into the digital environment just as other areas of business law have. The Government is about to pass new laws that will clarify many of the grey areas that exist at the moment regarding the validity of a contract that is signed on the Internet, and which has no physical element. Until then, contracts on the Internet are just as stringent as those that are signed on paper every day.

At the moment some simple steps can be taken to ensure that you have a valid claim against a contract if you need to go to litigation. Contracts can be order forms on a website or simply e-mail messages that have been exchanged between companies.

- Keep copies of all of your e-mail that relates to the contract. Also, if your contract relates to a specific part of your website, make a back-up copy of it before you amend it in any way.
- Make sure all terms and conditions are agreed upon. Today, it is simply a click of an 'agree' button in most cases when the small print is presented to a customer. Make sure that these terms are clearly understood.
- If you do business with a client on a regular basis, you may wish to ensure that they have a valid digital certificate that proves who they are, before entering into a contract.
- Payment method and currency should be clearly stated.
- Specify in which jurisdiction the contract is to be valid. The Internet may be a global marketplace, but you must still take into consideration the laws of other countries outside of your own. These could be very different, and may interpret your contract terms differently.
- If you are contracted to supply goods or services, remember that the usual terms in law still apply – see below for consumer protection law guidelines.
- Keep your website up-to-date. Misinformation can still be prosecuted against even on the Internet. The British Codes of Advertising and Sales Promotion still apply to online businesses. You must also ensure that you comply with the Data Protection Act – see below for more information.

Click-Wrap

This term relates to contracts that have been formed completely on the Internet. Most customers will have seen these contracts as they appear on websites before software or services are downloaded to the customer. The acceptance usually involves clicking on a button on the website labelled 'I Agree.'

The term originates from the shrink-wrapped software that is sold off the shelf today. Here, an agreement is entered into before the software packaging is opened. Once this is done, the supplier assumes the customer is willing to be bound by the contract for the use of the goods, in this case the software that will be installed on their computer.

Data Protection Act

Data is at the heart of any E-commerce business. The collection of customer details can be a great asset to any company that has an online presence. The UK protects the rights of individuals with the Data Protection Act of 1984. The Act gives rights to the individual who may have personal information about themselves held on computer systems. Individuals may:

- inspect the information that is held about them
- challenge this information, and claim compensation if appropriate.

The Act itself has eight Data Protection Principles.

1 Information obtained shall be processed lawfully and fairly.

2 Personal data shall be held only for one or more specified purposes.

3 Personal data held shall not be disclosed in any way that is incompatible with its fair and lawful use.

4 The data held shall be adequate, relevant, and not excessive in relation to the purpose it is being used for.

5 Personal data shall be accurate and, where necessary, kept up-to-date.

6 Data shall not be held for longer than is necessary for the purposes it is being used for.

7 An individual shall be entitled:
  - to be informed by the data user of the information that is held about them.
  - to access to any data held and, where appropriate, to have that data erased or corrected.

8 Appropriate security measures should be taken to protect data from unauthorised access, alteration, destruction or disclosure of information held.

The Act has now been updated to include new legislation, which is expected to come into force after April 1999. The 1998 amendments take into consideration the 1995 EC Data Directive which, in summary, provide:

- comparable levels of data protection across the EC
- the free flow of personal data
- full protection of the rights of European citizens
- the restricted transfer of personal information outside of the European Economic Area.

Generally, all of the principles of the 1984 Act have been retained. There are, however, some enhancements that need to be taken into consideration if your business retains personal information, which is then consequently processed further.

Subject access

Under the 1984 Act, the individual or data subject that the held data referred to had the right to access that data. The new Act goes much further in that the individual now has the right to:

- a full description of the data being processed
- a description of the purposes for which the data is being processed
- a description of any potential recipients of this data
- a description of the process that the information is subject to, if the data is to be processed automatically, and this may in turn significantly affect a decision about the individual; the individual will then have the right to an explanation of the logic behind the decision making process.

New rights

Under the new Act the data subject has the right to:

- prevent any processing of data that may cause distress or damage
- know the logic behind data processing methods
- not have significant decisions made by automated processes
- prevent data being processed for direct marketing purposes
- 'opt out' of having their data used
- compensation, which now can not only be claimed in the

event of damage as a result of inaccuracies or unauthorised disclosure, but also if distress has been caused – in this area the Act has been significantly extended.

Transfer of data overseas

In addition to the existing data protection principles, there is also a new principle that restricts the transfer of personal data outside of the EU. There are no restrictions on the transfer of data within member states, but data transferred outside of the EU may only take place to countries that have an 'adequate level of protection for the rights and freedoms of data subjects.'

As a consequence, businesses that have an Internet presence will have to think carefully when formulating their data handling policy. As the Internet is global, the transfer of data overseas and its security become of paramount importance. The new Principle that the EU Data Protection Directive has incorporated gives guidelines to data handlers. Data handlers should consider:

- the nature of the data
- the country of origin, and final destination of the data
- the law or any codes of conduct in force in the third country
- the security measures that are in use.

Complete details of all the above directives are available online from:

Data Protection: The Government's Proposals
www.hmso.gov.uk/acts/acts1998/19980029.htm

EU Data Protection Directive
www.homeoffice.gov.uk/datap1.htm

Data Protection Act of 1984
www2.echo.lu/legal/en/dataprot/dataprot.html

Consumer protection

The United Nations passed a resolution on the 9th of April 1985, that stated eight basic consumer rights:

- the right to safety
- the right to be informed
- the right to satisfaction of basic needs
- the right to choose
- the right to redress
- the right to consumer education
- the right to be heard
- the right to a healthy environment.

These basic human rights are particularly relevant in an E-commerce environment as they can be used as a framework for the design of an effective consumer strategy. In the following sections we will look at how each of these consumer rights applies to an online E-commerce business.

Consumer Credit Act of 1974
If a purchase is made via credit card and the item costs between £100 and £30,000, in the event that the goods are not delivered, the purchaser can claim against the credit card company as well as the supplier of the goods. Goods that are

bought outside of the UK may not fall within this legislation. The only course of action if the credit card company will not make a refund is an action against the supplier. Businesses, then, need to ensure that their goods and services are offered to their clients, as advertised, but more importantly that the goods can be delivered to the customer within a short space of time – we covered the logistical aspects of E-commerce on Friday.

Currently, the OFT (Office of Fair Trading) and the OECD (Organisation for European Cooperations and Development) are involved in a working party to build a set of guidelines that will cover four key areas of Internet trading.

Payment and redress
Secure payment systems, and means of resolving disputes.

Law enforcement
This will include the control of misinformation regarding goods and services.

Legal background
Including the legal status of electronic contracts, and product liability.

Privacy
Consumers' rights regarding security measures and personal and transaction data.

The Distance Selling Directive

The United Nations has already set out its charter on consumer rights protection in 1985. The Distance Selling Directive, adopted on 20 May 1997, aims to parallel this set of consumer rights in the EU. Member states have about three years to implement the Directive's main clauses. The Directive is very broad and any business that is involved in distance selling – which includes the Internet – must take steps to fulfil all of these criteria.

- *Consumers must be provided with basic information about the business they are dealing with.* This is quite basic and usually involves just name, address, characteristics of the goods or services, price, payments options, and rights to withdraw from the arrangement.
- *Written confirmation of the order.* The Directive states that the consumer must receive written confirmation of the goods or services that have been ordered in a 'durable medium.' The Directive recognises that e-mail is an acceptable means of confirmation.
- *Right to withdrawal.* The Directive gives consumers the right to withdrawal from a contract within seven working days without penalty, and without giving a reason.

- *Reimbursement.* The Directive requires that reimbursement should take place within 30 days.
- *Execution of order.* The supplier is required to fulfil an order placed within 30 days, unless the parties have agreed otherwise.
- *Cancellation or refund in the event of a credit card being used fraudulently.* Consumers will be able to request the cancellation of payments where their credit card has been used fraudulently.

Clearly, the new Distance Selling Directive has an impact on any E-commerce business. A simple rule of thumb is to apply the existing consumer law to your business, and make sure that you comply with all the Directive's clauses that apply to your type of business. The EU is quickly modifying existing laws to take on board the unique nature of the Internet as a new marketplace. Until a clear set of directives and laws are established, existing consumer law will apply to Internet trade.

At the end of the day it will not be up to bodies such as the OFT but those who wish to inspire the confidence of consumers to buy their wares to see that confidence grows.

(Source: Fiona Jayatilaka, Consumer Affairs Directorate)

Summary

Look closely at how your business is organised on the Internet at the moment, or think carefully about how you will transfer your business online if you haven't already done so. Consider the following points:

- Your customers are protected by consumer regulation when they buy from the high street, as well as on the Internet. Your business practices must comply with these laws.
- The Data Protection Act has now been updated to include the new Data Directive. Even if your business hasn't previously come under this Directive, the changes outlined above may now affect your business online.
- Many businesses that move online will apply existing marketing strategies to this new medium. Take care that these do not come into conflict with the new Distance Selling Directive.
- The Internet is awash with material that is tempting to use on a commercial website. Intellectual property rights as they apply to this material are still being ratified. Always seek legal advice before using any material on your website that may belong to a third party.
- Be clear on your business' tax situation in relation to the E-commerce element of your trade. As the Internet is an international medium, so international tax regulations need to be taken into consideration.
- The Euro – even though the UK has opted out for the present time – has to be taken into consideration by an online business. Business partners in Europe, as well as customers, will require any business that they trade with to be able to accept this currency. You must ensure that you have the correct procedures in place to handle this vital aspect of your business.

Action Plan

If you are about to embark on your first E-commerce venture then the Action Plan that is outlined below, though not a complete and detailed strategy, should allow any business to begin to plan for their digital future.

Step 1 Start thinking

Your business will use an electronic medium. Ask yourself:

- will your business sell products or services?
- will your business use the Internet channel as a means of supporting existing retail or service products?
- how will this new element of your business impact on the remaining organisation?
- how will this move affect your trading partners?

Step 2 Build your team

Your move to the Internet will undoubtedly impact on every area of your business. As a consequence of this, the team that designs your entry into the E-commerce environment must possess skills that span all of your company's activities.

> *We took people from the key processes and skills from around the business – marketing, emerging technology, operational management, content database; and we leveraged other skills including fulfilment and technical support. These people were taken out of their roles and put together in a dedicated project team in a separate building. We changed the environment, we changed what we wore (casual), we changed the tools we used to create an environment team ethic which stimulated creativity, and made constructive progress to agreed deadlines.*
>
> (Source: Julian Wright, Internet Marketing Manager, RS Components)

Step 3 Educate your business

You may decide that a dedicated team is needed to implement your plans for your website. The success of your Internet venture does, however, not stop there. Even though the rest of your business may not be directly involved with the E-commerce directive, they must still be educated in what the Internet means to their part of your company.

Step 4 Educate your partners and customers

Gone are the days when any business that entered the electronic marketplace simply gave out their website's URL and waited for customers. Today it is imperative that a business that is wholly based on the Internet, or has an E-commerce element to its organisation, should educate the customers they have with the knowledge they need to be able to interact with the business' website with the least amount of fuss. Similarly, business partners also need to be educated in your new business practices so the rewards that the Internet offers can be reaped by all members of the trading partnership.

Step 5 Assess your market

The Internet may be a completely new market for your business, or one that is intended to provide an ever increasing proportion of your business' income. Ask yourself:

- How many of your customers have access to the Internet at the moment?
- Is this from home, work or some other access point such as their local college or library?
- How sophisticated are your customers? Can they handle complex ordering procedures through their Internet access?
- Is there a market segment you could sell to as a test group? The information gained here would be invaluable when your E-commerce service is offered to a wider customer base.

- Can you maintain an E-commerce element to your business if sales are very small? Look closely at the economics of this sector of your business. Is it better to start small and build this element of your business over time, as the electronic marketplace grows?

These questions need to be answered if you are to design an E-commerce strategy that links closely with the market that you are either selling to at the moment or one that you hope to sell to in the future.

Step 6 Modify your distribution channels

If your business sells tangible goods, it will usually have a distribution channel already set up. In the digital marketplace, the distribution channel can be modified to reflect the move to the Internet or to enhance an existing strategy.

- Can any of your products be delivered electronically to your customers?
- If you sell only tangible products can you offer an added value to your customers' buying experience? UPS and FedEx allow their customers access to their tracking software – the progress of any package can be quickly ascertained.
- The current trend is to use existing channels for distribution of your products. Can you design new distribution channels that reflect your business and products?

Step 7 Streamline payment mechanisms

How do your customers pay for the goods that they buy
from you? If you have strategic alliances with other
suppliers, how do you each transfer cash between your
businesses? The Internet can add a completely new layer to
the payment mechanisms that you use. Consider:

- Can you continue with your existing payment systems
  without modification?
- How you can help your customers pay for your goods
  more easily and quickly.
- How to offer a completely secure method of payment –
  explain how encryption can make this a reality.
- How you can use electronic payment systems to
  streamline your purchases from other businesses. EDI
  now has an Internet facet which is bringing down the
  cost of implementation. Investigate if this system is
  suitable for your business, but don't install this system
  because another supplier simply insists on it – weigh the
  costs to benefits carefully.

Step 8 Customer support

As after sales support is imperative in the traditional
marketplace, this is even more so in electronic commerce.
Here, business can contact customers more easily, and
consequently customers can also contact your business
easily as well. Look closely at your existing customer
support strategy and implementation, and consider:

- how your presence on the Internet can help your existing customer support set up.
- can you use this new channel to offer a new channel of support?
- have you allocated the required human resources and budget to respond to an increase in customer support traffic once your website goes live?
- can you make this area of your business one of the best assets that your business has? When you have attracted a customer, you must retain that customer. Excellent after sales service is a prime means of achieving this.
- that the Web is a new marketplace for your customers. They expect something extra that isn't available in the high street, or through traditional distance selling means. A unique customer service is one way of making your business stand out from what is fast becoming a crowded marketplace.

Step 9 Assess your products

Traditionally, small easily shipped products have become bestsellers on the Internet. However, ask yourself:

- how well do your products sell on the Net?
- can you develop new products to sell on your site?
- can existing products be modified to give them a unique Web added value?
- have you given as much information about your products away on your website as possible? A customer may not need this information now, but they may in the future, which will bring them back to your website again and again.

Step 10 In-house design or outside contract

If your business is just embracing the new digital
marketplace with the introduction of an Intranet perhaps,
and is just beginning to consider the move to the Web, the
decision on whether you design this new channel yourself
or go outside of the company will be an important initial
step. Consider these points:

In-house

- You may feel that in-house is important for
  security reasons.
- Only you know your business in-depth.
- There may already be staff members who are
  Internet trained and can carry out the design and
  launch of your website.
- You may be able to build a prototype of your
  website, and then contract out the actual
  implementation to another company.
- You can install your own server on your premises.
  The costs of the server, support and maintenance,
  and qualified staff can become expensive. However,
  you will have complete control over your customers'
  access to your website.

Outsourcing

- A design agency will have a deeper understanding
  of the technical aspects of the Internet and can use
  the latest Web techniques to make your site unique.
- Set up can be much faster as an agency already
  has links with service providers such as Web page
  hosting companies and electronic payment
  processing services such as WorldPay.

- Faster implementation as a design agency will have staff whose skills cover all areas of Web design
- When problems occur the agency is on hand to resolve any technical difficulties.
- The maintenance of the site can be carried out by the agency or passed back to your company after the appropriate training.
- The agency will also be able to set up reporting and analysis software so you can track how well your website is doing in the marketplace.
- The agency will usually host your website on their own servers or have a very financially attractive partnership with a hosting company.

Step 11 Costs

Today, even the smallest business can have a Web presence
which can be as simple or as complex as they would like to
make it. The costs of entering the E-commerce arena fall
into a number of categories.

Hardware
- Server. Ideally you will need to buy your own server;
  maintenance and upgrades to your server have to be
  taken into consideration.
- Security is very important. Offering a completely secure
  online shopping environment is paramount. A good
  firewall is essential, but adds to your costs.

Content
You may intend to just use the E-commerce channel as
simply another means of selling to your customers. You
will, however, want to invest in the extra content that
makes your website unique. Consider:

- The content that you are using. Is it copyright free? Or
  has copyright clearance been granted for its use?
- If original content is to be created, make it clear to the
  agency that you contract to do the work what your exact
  requirements are. Treat this outsourcing as you would
  any other work that you currently tender to outside
  contractors.

Human resources
Most businesses that have not entered the electronic
commerce market will normally have to either recruit staff
to fill key roles such as the Webmaster of the site. You
should weigh up the following:

- Can any existing staff be retrained and seconded to the website design team?
- Draw up clear and precise outlines that detail the skills that you require before you approach an agency.
- Is it cost effective to allow all the maintenance of your site to be done via outsourcing?
- Can you strike a balance between the day-to-day running of your site which can be done in-house with existing staff, while at the same time letting an outside agency handle the more advanced and technical aspects of your website.
- Try and involve staff from all areas of your business. This is particularly important if your move to the Internet will impact on their responsibilities.
- Allow your staff to use their expertise where appropriate. You can enhance many skills that are already in place with education about how the Internet differs from a traditional retail environment; and thus can encourage the development of new ideas.

Step 12 The launch

The website is built. You are prepared for the extra customer support you will have to provide. The mechanisms that you will need to maintain the site are in place, so all there is left to do is to launch your website into the marketplace. As you would design and implement a campaign in the traditional marketplace so you should apply those principles to the Internet, while taking into consideration its unique features of course.

- Consider how you can use the established retail adage of 'location, location, location'. Forge strategic links with other companies that puts your company and its products before an audience in the correct location.

- Your brand name can be used as an excellent promotional tool. As you have spent a great deal of time building this in the traditional marketplace you can equally use this familiarity on your website. Extend this brand name with unique extras that are only available on your website.
- Use traditional marketing channels to promote your website. Press and other media can be used to draw potential customers to your new channel.
- Use the Web's versatility to the full, and the new channels that it offers. News groups, search engines, the proprietary online services such as AOL and CompuServe have a captive audience at whom you can aim appropriate advertising.

Summary

Today has looked closely at the practical aspects of setting up a business online. Generally consider these broad areas when you begin to develop your own strategy:

- The Internet is global. Always develop your website for a global audience. If your primary audience is in Europe, then the Single European Currency must be taken into consideration.
- Your goods and services will attract taxation in one form or another. Be aware of your liability as you move into an E-commerce based business.
- Your legal position should be clarified as much as possible. Again, as your market is on a global scale, you must consider the legal requirements of the markets you are selling to.

- Think carefully as you take each step in developing your own Action Plan. Each step needs to be meticulously planned and researched, and the business-wide implications need to be taken on board. If the Web is to be an extra marketing channel, and not your sole means of selling your products, how will this channel affect the rest of your business?

Finally, act now! The Internet will wait for no one. Access to a mass audience is taking shape. More and more shoppers will soon be willing to spend in the new electronic malls that the Internet is creating. No business can ignore the Internet and its potential commercial opportunities.